RECIPES FROM THE HEART

A COMPANION TO THE SAFEGUARDED HEART SERIES

MELANIE A. SMITH

WICKED DREAMS PUBLISHING

Copyright © 2018 by Melanie A. Smith
All Rights Reserved
Published by Wicked Dreams Publishing
Boise, ID
info@wickeddreamspublishing.com

This is a work of fiction. Names, characters, businesses, places, events, locales, and incidents are either the products of the author's imagination or used in a fictitious manner. Any resemblance to actual persons, living or dead, or actual events is purely coincidental.

Kindle eBook ISBN: 978-1-7328154-2-1
eBook ISBN: 978-1-7328154-9-0
Paperback ISBN: 978-1-7328154-3-8

Cover design © Wicked Dreams Publishing

BOOKS BY MELANIE A. SMITH

The Safeguarded Heart Series

The Safeguarded Heart

All of Me

Never Forget

Her Dirty Secret

Recipes from the Heart: A Companion to the Safeguarded Heart Series

The Safeguarded Heart Complete Series: All Five Books and Exclusive Bonus Material

Life Lessons: A series that can be read as standalones

Never Date a Doctor

Bad Boys Don't Make Good Boyfriends

You Can't Buy Love

The Heart of Rutherford: Life Lessons Novels 1 – 3

Standalone Romance Novels

Everybody Lies

Last Kiss Under the Mistletoe

Tough Love

Finding His Redemption

Short Stories

Cruising for Love

Hot for Santa

Anthologies

Heroes With Heat and Heart 2: A Charity Anthology

CONTENTS

Introduction	1

APPETIZERS
Focaccia	5
Bruschetta	7
Insalata Caprese	8
Stuffed Zucchini Flowers	10

SIDE DISHES
Baked Zucchini	15
Grandma D'Andreano's Stuffing	17

MAIN DISHES
Gnocchi	21
Fettucine Alfredo	23
Light Chicken Parmesan	25
Chicken Piccata	27
Pappardelle with Meat Sauce	29
Lasagna	31

DESSERTS
Panna Cotta	35
Tiramisu	37
New York Style Cheesecake	39

A Note from the Author	43
Acknowledgments	45
About the Author	47

INTRODUCTION

If you've read *The Safeguarded Heart Series*, you've probably figured out that I love food, Italian especially. It started with my family, having grown up with an Italian grandmother, amongst other family members, that instilled that love of food in me. My mother is a good cook too, but once I was out on my own I really fell in love with cooking for myself.

When I finished graduate school I treated myself to a trip to Italy. Part of that trip included a one-week cooking class in Tuscany through the Tuscan Women Cook program, which I highly recommend. For one week, I stayed in a small hotel in the gorgeous hilltop town of Montefollonico. Every morning we would receive a cooking lesson from a local restaurateur or the little old ladies that lived in the village and cooked at the hotel. We would eat what we made for lunch, then the afternoons would be filled with sightseeing, shopping, or cheese/wine tasting. Dinners were spent in restaurants scattered across Tuscany where we would spend the entire evening eating, drinking, and chatting. In one word, it was heaven. I learned to make pasta the Italian way. That their zucchini produced gorgeous, edible, delectable flowers. That nothing is better than the heavy fragrance of basil wafting through the air on a hot, sunbaked Tuscan summer afternoon.

In all, on that first visit I spent nearly a month exploring the country, often eating gelato twice a day, in additional to the bevy of other succulent dishes I sampled. Somehow, I still lost weight on that trip, though it might've been the ten or so miles I'd walk each day once I got to Rome. In any case, I was changed forever. I now knew what *real* Italian food tasted like.

That's not to diminish other Italian cuisines. Born and partially raised in New York, their Italian-American dishes are a powerhouse in their own right. And having also lived in California for many years, it also has its own spin on Italian favorites, which capture the best of the west coast with the decadence of Italy. My own cooking style has been vastly influenced by all three, and almost everything I cook ends up with Italian flavors.

While I'm no professional chef, I did hear from a number of readers that they drooled over the Italian dinner scene in the first book, so I figured I'd share those recipes. Because they're dishes I've actually made. And while I'm at it, I'll be sharing a few other dishes I love. Some are family dishes, some from Italian chefs I've picked up and made my own. Every single recipe is one I've tested and modified to my tastes over the years.

I'm also no professional cookbook writer but I'll do my best to lay everything out as best I can. In most cases these are simple, delicious meals that don't take all day to prepare. Because as much as I like to cook, I like to eat more, and I'm too impatient to wait that long. Either way, I hope you enjoy these recipes. From my kitchen, my heart, to yours.

"Recipes don't work unless you use your heart!"
—Dylan Jones

APPETIZERS

"All sorrows are less with bread."
—Miguel de Cervantes, Don Quixote

FOCACCIA

This deliciously dense and chewy bread is as versatile as it is tasty. It can be snacked on by dipping it in olive oil mixed with herbs or balsamic vinegar, it can be served with *antipasti*, it can be used as bread for paninis, or it can simply be served alongside a meal.

And while this is a basic recipe, it can also be dressed up to taste before baking by adding a light sprinkle of olives, onions, peppers, tomatoes, parmesan, or herbs such as thyme, rosemary, or sage. And though it has two rise cycles, it's exceedingly simple to make.

INGREDIENTS

- 1-1/3 cups warm water
- 1 envelope active dry yeast
- 3 tablespoons extra-virgin olive oil
- 3 1/2 cups all-purpose flour
- 2 teaspoons salt

. . .

DIRECTIONS

Combine water, yeast, and oil in a large bowl. Stir in flour and salt (can be done by hand or mixer). Once the dough comes together in a ball, knead it until it's smooth and elastic, about five minutes.

Put the dough into a lightly oiled bowl and cover with a damp cloth. Let rise until doubled, about an hour and a half.

Lightly oil a 9" x 13" pan. Press the dough into the pan until it's an even, flat layer. Cover with a damp cloth and let rise until doubled, about an hour and a half.

Preheat the oven to 425 degrees F. Dimple the dough with your (clean) finger every couple of inches, drizzle with olive oil, and sprinkle with salt.

Bake until golden brown, about 25 minutes. Number of servings varies by purpose, but generally makes about six servings.

BRUSCHETTA

nother simple recipe, this one actually does better with day-old bread, though the tomatoes should be top-notch for best flavor.

INGREDIENTS
 1 baguette
 2 lbs tomatoes
 4 garlic cloves
 Extra-virgin olive oil to taste
 Salt and pepper to taste

DIRECTIONS
 Slice bread and lightly grill on one side. Peel garlic and slice off one end. Rub garlic over the surface of the bread. Dice tomatoes and drizzle with olive oil. Sprinkle with salt and pepper. Toss to coat. Top the bread with the tomato when ready to eat. Serves 6-8.

INSALATA CAPRESE

Salad of Capri, in *tricolore,* the three colors of Italy. Served in the Italian dinner scene in *The Safeguarded Heart,* it's usually an *antipasto.* The ingredients are simple, but because of that the better quality the ingredients, the better the taste.

Ingredients
    4 large vine-ripened tomatoes
    1 lb fresh mozzarella loaf, drained
    1/4 cup fresh basil leaves
    Extra-virgin olive oil to taste
    Salt and pepper to taste

Directions
Slice the tomatoes and mozzarella in 1/4" thick slices. Arrange the tomato, mozzarella, and basil on a plate alternating and overlap-

ping. Drizzle with olive oil and sprinkle with salt and pepper. Makes 4-6 servings.

STUFFED ZUCCHINI FLOWERS

In *The Safeguarded Heart* I had these served as a first course, but these are more traditionally an appetizer (*antipasto*). I'd never had anything like it in the United States. I honestly didn't even know zucchini produced flowers, much less that they were edible and oh-so-delicious. I've ordered seeds from a U.S.-based Italian company so I can grow my own and dine on this delicious dish whenever I want!

INGREDIENTS
   15 oz can San Marzano tomatoes, crushed
   3 tablespoons olive oil
   1 tablespoons sugar
   1/4 cup water
   8 zucchini blossoms
   15 oz ricotta, drained
   1 egg
   3 tablespoons Parmesan cheese, grated
   1 tablespoon flat-leaf parsley, chopped

Pinch of nutmeg
Salt and pepper to taste

Directions

Heat olive oil in a large skillet over medium heat and add the tomatoes. Cook for half an hour. While the tomatoes stew, prepare the zucchini flowers by removing the centers then rinsing in cold water and patting dry. In a bowl, mix together the ricotta, egg, Parmesan, parsley, nutmeg, salt, and pepper. Use a small spoon or pastry bag to fill the flowers, cinching them closed with your fingers once nearly full (do not overfill).

Add sugar and water to tomatoes and stir. Add filled blossoms. Cook for 20 minutes on each side. Plate two blossoms, cover with tomato sauce. Serves 4.

SIDE DISHES

"You don't have to cook fancy or complicated masterpieces – just good food from fresh ingredients"
—Julia Child

BAKED ZUCCHINI

This dish is pure, cheesy, creamy, vegetable-y decadence. So much so that I usually serve it alongside a lighter entree, like a simple chicken dish.

Ingredients
- 2 lb zucchini
- 1 cup heavy whipping cream
- 1 cup mozzarella cheese, grated
- 1 cup fontina cheese, grated
- 1/2 cup Pecorino Romano cheese, grated
- 1 cup Italian breadcrumbs
- Salt and pepper to taste
- Extra-virgin olive oil to taste

Directions

Preheat the oven to 400 deg F. Grease a 9" x 12" baking dish. Slice the zucchini to finger-width. Line the pan with half of the zucchini. Sprinkle with salt and pepper. Drizzle half of the cream over the zucchini. Sprinkle with 1/2 cup each of mozzarella and fontina, 1/4 cup Pecorino Romano, then 1/2 cup of Italian breadcrumbs. Repeat with another layer. Drizzle or mist extra virgin olive oil lightly over the top. Bake until golden brown, about 30-35 minutes. Serves 4-6.

GRANDMA D'ANDREANO'S STUFFING

My great grandparents immigrated to New York after World War I from Pisciotta, Italy. I remember spending time with my feisty great grandfather, Daniel (Aniello) before he passed in 1989, but unfortunately my great grandmother, Teresa, passed away while my mother was pregnant with me, so I never had a chance to know her personally. But her legacy has lived on in the women of my family in many ways. Not least of which is through one of my most treasured holiday traditions — her stuffing recipe. In fact, it may be the only recipe I have that I know for sure came from her. I find that a bit odd since it's not strictly Italian, but it is amazing.

INGREDIENTS
- 1 bag seasoned stuffing mix
- 1 large onion
- 1/2 cup celery, diced
- 1/2 cup butter, melted
- 1 cup cheddar cheese, shredded

1 cup salami, diced
1 egg
1/2 cup Parmesan cheese, grated
Garlic salt to taste
Salt and pepper to taste
1 cup warm water

Directions

Melt the butter in a saucepan over medium heat. Add the onion and celery and cook until soft, about ten minutes.

Mix all ingredients in a large bowl and toss until well mixed. If using in a turkey, stuff loosely. Bake (extra or all) stuffing in a 9" x 12" pan, with giblets on top if you choose. Drizzle 1 cup of warm water over and bake uncovered in a 350 deg F oven until brown, about 20-25 minutes.

MAIN DISHES

"*Cooking is like love, it should be entered into with abandon or not at all.*"
—Harriet Van Horne

GNOCCHI

Gnocchi ... or as we sell them to our child who is, for some reason obsessed with Chinese dumplings ... Italian dumplings. Which they are, actually. Little plump pillows of potato-ey goodness covered in a delicious butter-thyme sauce.

INGREDIENTS
- 1/2 cup butter
- 1 tablespoon fresh thyme
- 1 lb russet potato
- 1/2 teaspoon salt
- 1/4 teaspoon pepper
- 1 egg, beaten
- 1/4 cup all-purpose flour
- 1/4 cup Pecorino Romano cheese, grated

DIRECTIONS

In a medium skillet, brown the butter over medium high heat for two minutes. Add the thyme leaves and remove from heat.

Poke the potato with a fork all over and microwave on high for six minutes. Turn over and microwave for another six minutes. Cut the potato open and remove the flesh with a spoon. Add salt, pepper, and egg and mix together. Add flour and mix together. Roll out chunks of dough into a finger-width rope and cut into 1/2"-1" pieces (depending on what size you like). You can lightly roll them under fork tines to give them a fancier look if you'd like.

Bring a large pot of water to a boil and cook the pieces until they float, then cook for another four minutes. Use a slotted spoon and transfer the gnocchi to the butter sauce and toss gently to coat. Serve topped with Pecorino Romano. Makes 4 servings.

FETTUCINE ALFREDO

One of my favorite indulgences. I pair it with sliced, roasted chicken and oven-roasted broccoli to balance out the insanely creamy, luscious sauce.

Ingredients
    2 cups heavy whipping cream
    1 lemon, juiced
    8 tablespoons butter
    2 teaspoons grated lemon zest
    Pinch of nutmeg
    1 lb fettucine
    1 cup Parmesan cheese, grated
    Salt to taste

Directions
    Put the heavy cream, lemon juice, and butter in a saucepan and

heat over medium, stirring until the butter melts completely. Stir in the lemon zest and nutmeg and set aside.

Cook pasta per directions on packaging (or 3-4 minutes for fresh pasta). Drain and return to pot. Add cream sauce and parmesan and mix over low heat until blended and pasta is fully coated with sauce. Season to taste and serve. Serves 8.

LIGHT CHICKEN PARMESAN

Chicken Parmesan is an Italian-American classic, but the breaded and fried version is too heavy for me, so I love this lighter take.

Ingredients

    4 slices of chicken breast, 1/4" thick
    2 tablespoons extra-virgin olive oil
    1 tablespoon fresh thyme leaves
    1 tablespoon fresh rosemary, chopped
    1 tablespoon fresh flat-leaf parsley, chopped
    Salt and pepper to taste
    1 cup tomato sauce
    1/2 cup mozzarella, shredded
    1/4 cup Parmesan, shredded

Directions

    Season the chicken on both sides with salt and pepper. Mix the oil and herbs together and brush onto both sides of the chicken. Heat an ovenproof skillet on medium-high heat and brown each chicken slice on both sides, just a minute or two per side. Turn off the heat and cover each chicken cutlet with tomato sauce. Sprinkle each with 1/4 of the mozzarella and parmesan. Put the pan in a 500 deg F oven and bake for 5-10 minutes until the chicken is cooked through. Serves 4.

CHICKEN PICCATA

I love the lemony-buttery sauce in this dish. The breading isn't overly heavy, and the pan frying keeps it on the lighter side as well. The lemon and parsley garnish makes this a very presentable — and delicious — dish.

Ingredients
- 4 slices of chicken breast, 1/4" thick
- 1/2 cup all-purpose flour
- 2 eggs, beaten
- 3/4 cup breadcrumbs
- 2 tablespoon extra-virgin olive oil
- 2 tablespoon butter
- 2 lemons, juiced
- 1 lemon, sliced into thin half-moons
- 2 tablespoons flat-leaf parsley, chopped
- Salt and pepper to taste

. . .

Directions

Salt and pepper both sides of the chicken breast slices. Prepare three plates, one each of flour, egg, and breadcrumbs. Heat the olive oil in a large skillet over medium heat. Coat the chicken on both sides in the flour, then the egg, then the breadcrumbs. Cook two minutes per side, then place on a large, lined sheet pan. Once all chicken slices are pan-cooked, place the sheet pan in a 425 deg F oven for 5-10 minutes.

Wipe out the pan you used to brown the chicken. Melt the butter over medium heat. Add the lemon juice, and salt and pepper to taste. Boil for a few minutes until the mix has reduced by half.

Top each chicken breast with a lemon slice, a sprinkling of flat leaf parsley, and a generous pour of sauce. Serves 4.

PAPPARDELLE WITH MEAT SAUCE

Another dish from the Italian dinner scene in the *The Safeguarded Heart*, the first time I had this was actually with boar meat (and fresh pasta, of course). I was trepidatious to say the least. Much to my surprise, it was delicious.

Pappardelle is less common here, but this wide, flat noodle holds sauce like a champ. My favorite is De Cecco. The sauce recipe takes some time, but it's totally worth it, and also multiplies nicely.

Ingredients

- 1 lb Pappardelle pasta
- 2 tablespoons extra-virgin olive oil
- 1 onion, diced
- 2 carrots, diced
- 2 stalks celery, diced
- 2 cloves garlic, minced
- 1/2 cup flat-leaf parsley, chopped
- 1 lb. ground beef and/or pork

28 oz can San Marzano tomatoes, crushed
1 cup tomato sauce
1/2 cup red wine
2 tablespoons tomato paste

Directions

Heat the olive oil in a large pot over medium heat and add onion, carrot, and celery, sautéing until translucent, about 10 minutes. Add garlic and parsley and cook another three minutes.

Add meat and red wine. Break up meat and cook through, about 10 minutes.

Add crushed tomatoes and tomato paste. Mix well and cook until bubbling. Lower heat to medium-low and cook for two to three hours, until the sauce is a rich, dark color.

Cook pasta according to package directions. Portion and ladle sauce over pasta. Serves 6-8.

LASAGNA

This Italian-American staple appears briefly in *All of Me* (*The Safeguarded Heart Series Book* 2). But even if it hadn't, I can't imagine putting together a list of my favorite recipes without including lasagna. I even served it at my own wedding. It's always a crowd pleaser!

INGREDIENTS

    2 lb ground beef or pork
    1 onion, diced
    2 cloves garlic, chopped
    2-15 oz cans diced tomatoes
    2-15 oz cans tomato sauce
    1 tablespoon Italian seasonings
    1 box lasagna noodles
    2 eggs, beaten
    32 oz ricotta
    1 cup Parmesan cheese, grated
    1-1/2 cup mozzarella, shredded

Directions

Heat a large pot over medium-high heat. Cook the meat, onion, and garlic until browned. Stir in undrained tomatoes, tomato sauce, and seasoning. Boil and simmer, covered, for 15 minutes, stirring regularly.

Cook lasagna noodles per the directions on the box while the sauce simmers, drain, and set aside.

In a large bowl, mix ricotta, egg, and 1/2 cup Parmesan cheese.

Using a large lasagna pan (~10" x 16") layer sauce on the bottom, then line with slightly overlapped noodles. Top with half of the cheese filling, smoothing into an even layer. Top with half of the meat sauce, smoothing into an even layer. Top with half of the mozzarella. Repeat. Sprinkle the top with the remaining 1/2 cup of parmesan.

Bake at 375 degrees F for 45-50 minutes, until heated through. Easily serves 10-12.

DESSERTS

"Life is uncertain. Eat dessert first."
—Ernestine Ulmer

PANNA COTTA

The Italian dinner in *The Safeguarded Heart* featured a *Panna Cotta* with berries for dessert. I'll be honest. No matter how hard I try, I can't get this dessert to have the exact smooth texture of the one I had my first night in Italy. But you know what? It's pretty close, and still freaking delicious. Creamy, sweet, and rich, it really does need the balance of fresh berries, so top with your favorite and enjoy!

INGREDIENTS
- 1 cup whole milk
- 1 envelope unflavored gelatin
- 3 cups heavy whipping cream
- 1/3 cup sugar
- 1/2 teaspoon vanilla extract
- 2 cups fresh berries

DIRECTIONS

Put the milk in a pan, then sprinkle the gelatin on top and let sit for five minutes. Stir constantly over medium heat for five minutes until the gelatin dissolves, but the milk does not boil. Add the remaining ingredients and stir for a few minutes, until the sugar dissolves. Remove from the heat and whisk until its lukewarm (you can do this over an ice bath to speed it up). Then divide into eight 1/2 cup ramekins or glasses. Refrigerate overnight to let the dessert set. Top each with 1/4 cup fresh berries immediately before serving. Serves 8.

TIRAMISU

Literally "lift me up" in Italian, this dessert is one of the most quintessential of Italian confections. And this variant is my hands-down favorite. It uses a rather non-traditional biscuit (or cookie as we Americans call it) that I order from Amazon.com. You plate it in large scoops, so this is not so much the "pretty" kind that you'll take pictures of, but it is out-of-this-world delicious.

Ingredients

- 4 eggs, separated
- 5 tablespoons sugar
- 12 oz mascarpone
- 2.5 oz espresso
- 3/4 cup Vin Santo or other dry, white dessert wine
- 1 package Pavesini biscuits (or ladyfingers)
- 4 oz dark chocolate, chopped into small chunks

. . .

Directions

Mix the egg yolks and sugar in a mixer until pale and fluffy, about 5-7 minutes. In a separate bowl, whisk the mascarpone until it's light and fluffy. In a third bowl, whisk the egg whites until they form soft peaks. Fold the mascarpone into the egg whites, then fold that mixture into the yolk/sugar mix.

Mix the Vin Santo and espresso together. Dip the Pavesini in the mixture, lining a large bowl or dish with half of the biscuits. Cover with half of the filling. Place another layer of dipped biscuits on top, then cover with the remaining filling. Note, depending on the shape of the bowl/dish you may need to modify to more layers. Cover with the chocolate chunks, then chill in the refrigerator for 2-4 hours for the dessert to set. Makes 6-8 servings.

NEW YORK STYLE CHEESECAKE

I love this recipe because it's the easiest I've found, with no water bath required. I actually danced around my apartment with happiness the first time I tasted this cheesecake. I also had an at-home baking business for a few years and this was my absolute best-seller. You can top it with berries, chocolate, whipped cream, or just eat it plain. Any way you slice it (see what I did there?), it's ah-mazing.

INGREDIENTS

Crust:
2 cups graham cracker crumbs
4 tablespoons sugar
6 tablespoons unsalted butter, melted

Filling:
2 lb. cream cheese
1-1/4 cup sugar
4 eggs
1/2 cup sour cream

1 teaspoon vanilla extract

Directions

Adjust the oven rack to the middle and preheat the oven to 450 degrees F.

Mix the crust ingredients well until the graham cracker crumbs are uniformly moist, then press them into the bottom and sides of a 9 inch springform pan.

Beat the cream cheese with an electric mixer until light and fluffy (it gets there faster if you let the cream cheese come to room temperature first). Beat in the sugar completely. Beat in the eggs one at a time. Beat in the sour cream and vanilla. Scrape the sides and continue beating until everything is thoroughly mixed, then pour the mixture into the crust.

Bake for 15 minutes, then lower the temperature to 200 degrees F and open the oven door completely for a few minutes before closing it back up and baking until the edges are set, but the middle still wiggles, which will take around an hour.

Cool on a rack to room temperature, then refrigerate for at least four hours, preferably overnight, before topping and serving. Makes 10-12 servings.

Want more? Check out Melanie A. Smith's latest release *Finding His Redemption: An Enemies to Lovers Rock Star Romance*
https://melanieasmithauthor.com/books-finding-his-redemption.html

Sign up for Melanie A. Smith's newsletter to get a FREE book plus all the latest news and more
https://mailchi.mp/melanieasmithauthor.com/nlsignup

A NOTE FROM THE AUTHOR

Thank you so much for reading! Now ... I need your help! Will you please take a minute to leave a review? It doesn't have to be long — just a couple sentences saying what you thought of the book on any retailer, goodreads, and/or BookBub. Your opinion is important to me, and for potential readers. Thank you!

ACKNOWLEDGMENTS

First love goes to my mother, who taught me to cook. Next, my college roommates, who were my first real guinea pigs. And now to my wonderful husband, who will eat and love just about anything I put in front of him.

A huge thanks to the wonderful people at Tuscan Women Cook for providing the experience of a lifetime, with especially fond memories of Bill Sutherland, one of the kindest people I've ever met, may he rest in peace.

And of course, to my favorite chefs who inspired me the whole way - Emeril Lagasse, Giada DeLaurentiis, Ina Garten, Jamie Oliver, and so many more. And to those who made me think more about what I'm putting in my mouth - Michael Pollan, Jo Robinson, and my foodie-est friends.

And finally, to Angela Belli, my friend and most favorite Italian chef, with whom I can talk food, Italy, and being a woman in business.

ABOUT THE AUTHOR

Melanie A. Smith is an award-winning and international best-selling author of steamy contemporary romance fiction. A voracious reader and lifelong writer, Melanie's writing began at a young age with short stories and poetry. After college and a career as an aircraft engineer, she shifted to domestic engineering and property management and eventually found a balance where she was able to return to writing fiction. Melanie is also a Mensan and enjoys spending time with her family, cooking, and driving with the windows down and the stereo cranked up loud.

facebook.com/MelanieASmithAuthor
twitter.com/MelASmithAuthor
instagram.com/melanieasmithauthor

www.ingramcontent.com/pod-product-compliance
Lightning Source LLC
Chambersburg PA
CBHW030202100526
44592CB00009B/398